BUILTH WELLS

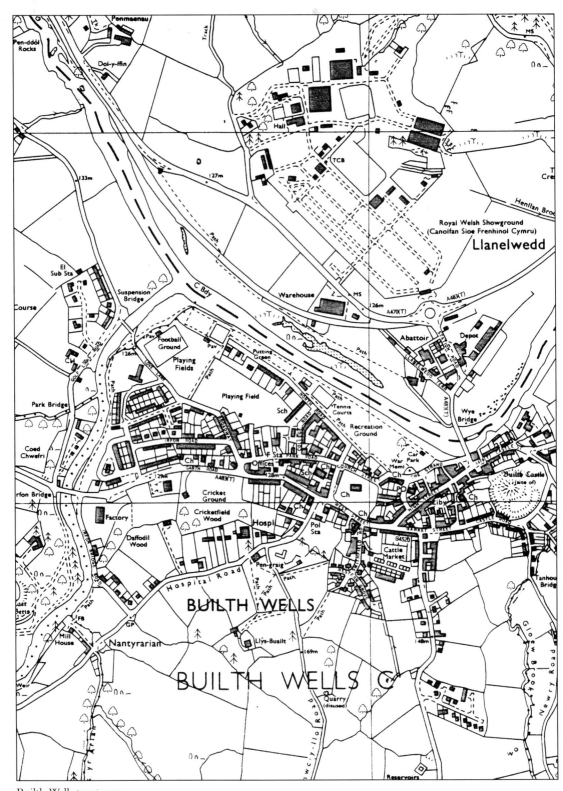

Builth Wells town map
(Reproduced from the Ordnance Survey map with the sanction of the Controller of HM Stationery Office. Crown Copyright Reserved.)

Towns and Villages
OF WALES

BUILTH WELLS

J.B. SINCLAIR
AND
R.W.D. FENN

ALAN SUTTON

First published in the United Kingdom in 1993 by
Alan Sutton Publishing Limited
Phoenix Mill · Far Thrupp · Stroud · Gloucestershire

First published in the United States of America in 1993 by
Alan Sutton Publishing Inc · 83 Washington Street · Dover · NH 03820

British Library Cataloguing in Publication Data

Sinclair, J.B.
Towns and Villages of England and Wales:
Builth Wells/Llanfair ym Muallt
I. Title II. Fenn, R.W.D.
942.956

ISBN 0-7509-0490-9

Library of Congress Cataloging in Publication Data applied for

Typeset in 11/13 Bembo.
Typesetting and origination by
Alan Sutton Publishing Limited.
Printed in Great Britain by
Hartnolls Ltd, Bodmin, Cornwall.

Contents

Preface

This book grew from a course of lectures given in Builth Wells High School in the autumn of 1992 for the Department of Extra-Mural Studies of the University College of Wales, Aberystwyth. We would like to record our gratitude to some of our students who have most generously put their knowledge and treasures at our disposal. Thus, we have drawn deeply not only upon the extensive collection of photographs and postcards of Mr T.E. Turner, Registrar of Births and Deaths for the Builth Wells registration district, but also upon his lifelong knowledge of the town. Mrs Gwen Davies has been most helpful, giving us tactful advice and looking at our manuscript, saving us from several errors of fact. Dr Colin Hughes, Head of the History Department at Builth High School, has shared his knowledge of the school's history with us. The staff of Powys Archives, especially Mr Alun Edwards, have always made us welcome, as has Mr Martin Bidgood of Powys County Planning Department. Besides using the traditional sources available to the local historian in archives and libraries, we have also profited from a study of Mr Malcolm Morrison's *Pictorial History of Builth Wells*, published under his own initiative in 1989. For errors of fact, omissions, and hurt feelings, of which we hope there are not too many, we take full responsibility and offer our sincerest apologies.

J.B. SINCLAIR
R.W.D. FENN
Kington, July 1993

CHAPTER ONE

Market Town or Spa?

Builth, or Buellt as it is in Welsh, is thought to have belonged originally to the country of which it became the administrative centre. The administrative and territorial unit of medieval Wales was the *cantref*, which in theory consisted of a hundred townships, and its origins lie in the ancient Welsh kingdoms. The *cantref* of Buellt lay between the Wye and the Tywi and occupied all of what was to become the old county of Brecon north of the Eppynt, an area of some 174 square miles.

It was conquered by the Normans in about 1095 by Philip de Breos who built a timber motte-and-bailey castle, strategically placed to control the ancient crossing of the Wye, the route to the south over the Eppynt to Brecon, and the entrance to the Irfon valley which gave access to the west. A settlement grew up around the castle and a church was founded, dedicated to Our Lady. It was from this church that the infant township took its name, Llanfair ym Muallt, the Church of Our Lady in Buellt. In time this became abbreviated to Buellt in Welsh and Builth in English.

Builth returned to Welsh rule in 1229 after the marriage of Dafydd ap Llywelyn, the first Prince of Wales, to Isabella de Breos. It was, however, captured for the English crown in 1241, but not for long, and in 1260 it was seized by Llewelyn ap Gruffydd (*c.* 1225–82), Llewelyn the Last, and razed to the ground. But in 1277 Edward I rebuilt it in stone and granted the borough of Builth a royal charter. The strategic importance of the castle was reflected in Edward I's choice of James of St George as its architect. It was the precursor of a series of castles Edward I was to begin in North Wales during his campaign of 1282.

The fortifications of the new castle included a dominating great tower, surrounded by a stone curtain wall interspersed with six towers, a drawbridge flanked by two more towers, and a stone wall and ditch two metres deep to the inner bailey. It was intended that the outer bailey should also have a stone wall, but in 1282 the work was incomplete when Llewelyn the Last made his final bid for Welsh independence which led to his death at Cilmeri. Harassed by the English, he was denied refuge in Builth castle, for which the jibe *bradwyr Buallt*, the traitors of Builth, was used for ever after against the people of the town. He now made his way westward up the Irfon valley, still pursued

Builth castle as it may have appeared in 1227

by the English who engaged him in battle by the Irfon near Llanynys church. Llewelyn was killed and his head was sent for exhibition to London. His body was eventually buried at the great Radnorshire Cistercian monastery at Abbey Cwm Hir.

The twentieth century has seen a revival of interest in Welsh history and a revival of national awareness. Amends have been made for the manner of Llywelyn's death and the subsequent neglect of his memory. In 1902 a 12-foot obelisk of Llanelwedd stone was erected at Cilmeri by Stanley Price Morgan Bligh, the local squire. It was replaced in 1956 by the present monument of granite quarried from Llywelyn's native Gwynedd, and bears the inscription: *Ger y fan hon y Lladdwydd Llywelyn ein Llyw olaf 1282* – near this spot was killed our Prince Llywelyn 1282.

Builth castle was again besieged in 1294 and in 1301 it was given to Edward, Prince of Wales, later Edward II. Eventually it became part of the patrimony of the Mortimers, the Earls of March. It may have resumed some importance at the beginning of the fifteenth century during the revolt of Owain Glyndwr 'to free the Welsh people from the slavery of their English enemies'. He enjoyed some local support and it is recorded how in November 1401 men in the Builth region forfeited their property because of their 'insurrection'. After Glyndwr the castle sank into gradual decline and ruin, so that now all that remains of it, as it languishes in obscurity behind the

The 1902 obelisk to Llywelyn the Great at Cilmeri

Its 1956 successor

All that now survives of the castle

Lion Hotel, are its substantial earthworks. Meanwhile, Builth was troubled by ills for which a castle was no protection.

One of these ills was plague, which seems to have assaulted Builth in the 1350s. Thus the *Cambrian Traveller's Guide* informed visitors to the town in 1813 that: 'About one mile west of the town runs a small brook called Nant yr Arian, or Money Brook, from a tradition that when the plague raged in Builth, provisions were put down here, and the country people were paid for them by money dropped into the water.'

Another and recurring ill was that of fire. In December 1691 (though some say it was 1690), 'half the town was consumed by fire'. It is said to have 'raged for five hours, consuming the dwellings of forty substantial families, with all their corn, furniture, effects and merchandises, to the great impoverishment of the adjacent country, and the decay of trade'. Damage was put at £10,780. A further loss of £2,000 was sustained by those who felt the need to seek relief. Many buildings in Builth, surrounded as it is with well-wooded hills, were, of course, timber-framed under thatch, and burned merrily.

Through the endeavours of Sir Rowland Gwynne (1660–1726) of Llanelwedd, who represented various constituencies in parliament for a period of twenty-three years and was knighted by Charles II in 1680, the Crown granted letters patent, whereby the homeless could circulate a petition for assistance throughout the kingdom. This was a common practice before the emergence of insurance companies and fire insurance policies.

A photograph exists of a receipt, recording that the minister and churchwardens of an unidentifiable parish in Lincolnshire received from their parishioners the sum of $1\frac{1}{4}$ d. for 'the Relief of the poor Sufferers of Builth in the County of Brecon, towards their great Loss by Fire'. Unfortunately, despite the generosity of the people of Lincolnshire, the parishioners of Builth derived little benefit and some complained that the money 'was shamefully misapplied by the collectors and laid out at interest by them for their own benefit'.

When it came to the rebuilding of the town, Edward Price of nearby Maesmynis was appointed surveyor. His house there, Abercneiddon, was built of brick, and far more fire-resistant than its timber-framed predecessor. Since brick-built houses are rare in Breconshire before the mid-nineteenth century his choice of material may well be related to Builth's great fire. Brick was also chosen (though roughcast rendering now conceals the fact), for the High Street building of five bays, now occupied in part by the White Horse Hotel. Some think this was, in fact, the only house built from the proceeds of the royal brief.

A source of more readily available and cheaper building material was provided by the stone of the decaying castle, whose military career was by now long over. Timber-framed houses which had survived the fire were refronted in castle stone and new houses were built of it entirely. Little evidence, though, has survived of any systematic rebuilding of the town having taken place under the influence of Edward Price. At the end of the eighteenth century it still 'consisted principally of one long street, formed of a connected chain of shops and public houses'.

Notwithstanding these criticisms, the town had acquired some handsome houses of modest size, several of which have survived Victorian redevelopment to give us some idea, for example, why when the Revd Richard Warner of Bath passed through Builth in August 1797 he thought the town 'small and neat'. He did not stop, however, 'for it contains nothing that deserves particular attention'. It was the river which attracted him: 'Here we first met with the celebrated river Wye, on the banks of which the town is built.' The same year saw a visit from Samuel Ireland, the engraver, who commemorated his visit with a tinted engraving of the town. Seven years later Sir Richard Colt Hoare (1758–1838), the antiquary and historian, was in the

The town as Sir Richard Colt Hoare saw it in 1805

town. His line engraving of a view of Builth was published in 1805. But it was the scenic setting of the river, the bridge, and the wooded hills beyond which most attracted the tourist's attention.

In 1801 Builth had a population of 677 living in 108 houses. The long, low, two-storeyed eighteenth-century Old Hall in West Street held little appeal for the traveller, but there were several pleasing little town houses like Strand House near the river. Sadly it is nowadays disguised as a building society, but until recently it had stone quoins and the date 1756 on its pediment. The Builth lawyer Thomas Price lived here. A justice of the peace and deputy lieutenant of Breconshire, he was the county's undersheriff in 1791.

A little further down the road opposite Alpha chapel is Llanfair House. This handsome, solid, stone-built villa has a pillared Tuscan porch. At one time a Dr Hugh Bennet lived here and thereby displayed the success of his medical practice. The house was erected in 1820, a year which saw the publication of a coloured aquatint engraving of Builth by Theodore Fielding (1781–1851), after a picture by his kinsman, Copley Fielding. Llanfair was not

The seventeenth-century Old Hall in West Street

The Lion Hotel, patronized by Lady Hesther Stanhope in 1808

the first house of that name on that site; in 1788 one John Lawrence, 'attorney-at-law', was living there. The Lion Hotel facing the bridge at the other end of the town belongs to the same period. It was the principal inn in the town.

Cefn Dyrys, alias Wellfield House, 'the noble mansion' of the Thomas family

Two other houses, both in West Street, would also have won the contemporary tourist's approval. Hafod, with its elegant Venetian windows, is another early nineteenth-century house to which a pair of Victorian bay windows have been added, somewhat masking its original proportions. A very similar house, but without the additions, was demolished in 1936 to make way for the new post office. Near Hafod is Peterwell, with a pair of delicately proportioned two-storey Regency bows. Its demure modesty belies the status of some of its occupants. In 1857 Thomas Jones, who then lived in it, agreed to sell The Bwlch at Llanddewi in north Radnorshire to Sir John Benn Walsh, who owned the Llanddewi estate, for the then not inconsiderable sum of £1,150.

The last early nineteenth-century topographer to visit the town was Thomas Roscoe (1791–1871), whose *Wanderings and Excursions in Wales*, published in 1836 and 1837, eventually brought him to Builth. Like others before him he deemed it to be: 'Finely and picturesquely situated, and, seen from any of the surrounding heights, [it] looks pretty enough; but on a nearer inspection, the streets prove narrow and zigzag, and contain but few good houses. . . . From one end of the town to the other, is a continuation of shops and public houses.'

TAKING THE WATERS

In the eighteenth century taking the waters at spa towns either out of medical necessity or for social pleasure became highly fashionable and spas of varying sophistication blossomed all over Britain, Bath setting the standard. Central Wales, despite its remoteness and inaccessibility, was no exception to this, and in 1748 the *Gentleman's Magazine* exclaimed:

> Let England boast Bath's crowded springs,
> Llandrindod happier Cambria sings.

In 1756 Dr Wessel Linden, a physician whose qualifications have proved difficult to verify, published his *Treatise on the Three Medicinal Mineral Waters of Llandrindod in Radnorshire, South Wales*. The presence of mineral waters in the vicinity of Llandrindod had been known since 1696 and local people had resorted to them for what was seen as their curative properties. The hunt for further mineral springs was on; Llandrindod was fast developing as a spa and since its early days, some of its visitors had to stay at Builth, seven miles away, because of the shortage of accommodation in the new town. When mineral springs were discovered near Builth at the Park and Glanne Wells a new career seemed to await the town.

In March 1747 Richard Morris, one of three famous brothers from Anglesey, came to Builth and tasted the waters, 'noted for curing certain

Park Wells: pump house and visitors' accommodation

Glanne Wells: pump house and pavilion

distempers by washing and taking inwardly . . . Good for asthma and disease of the lungs . . . it tastes strongly of sulphur and smells like gunpowder'.

The *Cambrian Traveller's Guide* found in 1813 that 'the *Park Wells*, situated upon the northern extremity of a large forest, about a mile distant from the town, are a considerable attraction. They consist of three mineral springs; the first is saline, the second sulphurous, and the third chalybeate. Over the Pump Room is a neat and commodious appartment in which the visitors occasionally amuse themselves with dancing.' This pump house was a pretty little two-storied octagonal building with a pointed roof, and a guest house beyond. This accommodation, along with that offered elsewhere in the district, was deemed in tourist guides to be less than adequate. Thus in 1842 Lewis's *Topographical Dictionary of Wales* complained: 'Though from their well established reputation they would be a powerful attraction to visitors, yet no more than three or four houses in the town or neighbourhood are found which offer any accommodation. . . .'

The Glanne Wells were rather less sophisticated and required an even greater degree of stamina and athleticism than their rivals at the park. 'To reach the Glanne Wells, the main road is followed for some distance to the westward. Soon after passing a bridge over the river Irfon, a *stile* is reached on the right side of the road, which leads to the pump-room, *a pleasantly situated cottage*. The wells here are chalybeate and sulphur.' Pavilions were later built at both wells, wherein the waters could be drunk in comfort and ease.

The proprietor of Park Wells enterprisingly bottled the waters for sale and claimed it would keep for years, remaining as clear as crystal, undergoing no change, and retaining its freshness during the hottest weather. It certainly had its devotees and in October 1896 a Builth resident committed to paper the benefits to be derived from the saline water from Park Wells:

> It is as good when bottled as when taken from the spring, and can safely be taken winter and summer alike. I often, in winter, get out of bed and swallow a tumblerful of the water and go back to bed again for a short while, and find this a very agreeable way of taking it in cold weather. It is my family medicine. We all take it summer and winter, and would not be without a jar full of it, handy for use, on any account. Bottled in three half-pint wine bottles, properly sealed, is the proper way of keeping it. It is a powerful aperient, but does not gripe. It is very useful as an injection for piles. It is also an excellent cosmetic; and it may even be applied to babies for nettle-rash, sores, &c.

The spa's devotees displayed touching loyalty to it even when medicine was on the threshold of the penicillin age. Thus in May 1927 Mr Moses Russell of Plymouth was moved to write to the proprietor of Park Wells: 'I feel that I must . . . let you know the wonderful benefit I have received through taking the Builth Wells Saline and Sulphur Waters. I was crippled with peritonitis of the knee and thought I should have to give up my career as a professional footballer, but since taking your wonderful waters I have not only played in every match last season, but am still fit and have had no recurrence of the trouble.'

But, alas, medical endorsement was not sufficient to establish Builth Wells in the face of the opposition provided by its far more successful rival at Llandrindod. It never attracted the distinguished clientele that made its way to Llandrindod, a spa which saw itself as the Buxton or indeed Montpellier of South Wales. The early nineteenth-century trickle of aristocratic visitors to Builth gave way, with the advent of the railway, to a stream, rather than a flood, of less socially distinguished visitors.

In 1903 the potential visitor was advised:

> Builth is quite a nice little town in itself, and beyond a doubt is most delightfully as well as conveniently situated, but I would advise an intending visitor to avoid the actual holiday season, when it is given over to

'Builth is quite a nice little town.' Broad Street unusually empty

the Joes and Jills of the Glamorgan collieries, who flock hither to drink the most potent saline water that the heart of a dyspeptic could desire, and to wash it down, when the day's *regime* is over, with generous libations of *Cwrw dda*.

LEISURE AND PLEASURE

What, indeed, could the visitor to Builth do to pass his time? The restoration of Builth parish church in 1875 would have seen the introduction of an organ, if there was not one already, and the final disappearance of the church band. Other organs would have followed, as the town's chapels were progressively rebuilt or enlarged to accommodate the growing number of summer visitors to the spa of Builth Wells. Hymn-singing was one of the pleasures enjoyed by these visitors in compensation for the discomforts incurred in drinking the medicinal waters. Sermon-tasting could also be indulged in at the same time as hymn-singing, and one tourist noted, with the voice of the connoisseur, that 'the preachers are here in force at all times'.

In 1890 congregations at Builth were able to sing a new hymn-tune, named after the town. This 'powerful and popular hymn-tune' was composed by David Jenkins (1848–1915), who became Professor of Music at the

Builth Wells Male Voice Choir, 1927

University College of Wales at Aberystwyth in 1910. It is usually associated with the words *Rhagluniaeth y nef* (The Providence of Heaven) by the Welsh Methodist hymn-writer David Charles, though in Builth it is sung to words written by Mrs J.W. Phillips, wife of one of Alpha Chapel's ministers.

Another pleasure was the occasional *eisteddfod*, or concert, at which Builth and District Harmonic Society's choir, under conductor Mr Evans (better known as Llew Buellt), would sing. The choir was very successful at *eisteddfodau* even at a national level, coming first, for example, at Llandudno in 1896 and at Blaenau Ffestiniog in 1897. At one time choral singing was so popular in the district that it could sustain two choirs, the rival one being conducted by Mr A.P. Morgan, though prudence and necessity eventually brought about their amalgamation. In more recent times the Women's Institute choir and the Côr Dyffryn Gwy have carried on the town's choral tradition.

Amateur concerts were also popular, at least with townsfolk, and raised funds for good causes with their proceeds. In 1870 those who were responsible for finding funds for the restoration of the parish church gratefully received the £50 which a concert given by local musicians produced. Likewise, gas was installed in the Endowed Schoolroom in 1876 with the help given by another such concert. Visits from professional entertainers were rare,

The Builth pageant, 1909

though in 1866 the town's Literary Institution was able to attract the services of Mme E.L. Williams, an esteemed singer, for their musical entertainment, *Life and Character*. Reserved seats cost half a crown and the unreserved a shilling.

The amateur musician was able to resort to Howard Lewis, bookseller, stationer, and music-seller, who always had accordions, concertinas, and violins in stock. Alternatively they could go to the commercially versatile J.H. Probert, who functioned in the Market Hall buildings as a hairdresser, tobacconist, and cycle agent, while also having in stock 'Phonographs and Disk-Talking Machines'. And if, like Kilvert, they derived great pleasure from musical boxes, they could always take them to Mr Putley, the High Street watchmaker, to be cleaned and repaired. In 1900 the services of Mr John Roberts of Market Street were available for those seeking a professional harpist.

In the first half of the nineteenth century companies of strolling players made their way to Builth, the Old South Wales Company, for example,

The Boating Pavilion in the Groe

putting on *Charles II or The Merry Monarch* in July 1826. In 1842 W.W. Dunant's strolling company from North Wales also played in the town. In 1909 the history of the town and district was portrayed in a most ambitious pageant involving hundreds of amateur players, and apparently attracting thousands of onlookers.

In 1903 a visitor noted that 'between the town and the river is a delightful grassy strip of common land where the inhabitants of Builth, on Sundays and holidays, disport themselves.' This is the Groe, which once served as a village green to which animals were taken daily to graze. It also served as a rubbish dump and played its part in the town's tanning business, as there was access through the Groe to the Tanner's Pool in the Wye. By 1892 the custom of boys bathing naked at the bridge had been suppressed. There was, instead, a boating pavilion in the Groe and a landing-stage for the construction of a weir across the river had made boating possible. Rowing boats could be hired by the hour and tennis and bowls were played. At the turn of the century the Groe's charms were further enhanced by the planting of trees along the riverside, now a handsome part of the landscape. Originally, however, the trees were known as Abram's folly, Mr Abram Davies being the local councillor through whose initiative they were planted. Boating on a more modest scale was also possible on the Irfon near its confluence with the Wye,

15

Boating on the Irfon

which was given to flooding. On occasion, skating was a winter pleasure. In the late nineteenth century Builth was also known as a centre for otter-hunting.

Many visitors enjoyed exploring the surrounding countryside by bicycle, despite its undulations and poor roads. The Lion Hotel advertised itself as the local headquarters of the Cyclists' Touring Club, and Mr Jarman's Cambrian Cycle and Motor Depot offered the discriminating cyclist, for sale or hire, 'Humber, Rudge, Whitworth, Royal Enfield, Quadrant, & Hazelwood cycles'. He would also undertake 'repairs of all kinds with Promptitude and Skill'.

For those whose pleasures were even more muscular, Builth Rugby Football Club was founded in 1882. The Cricket Club followed in 1884 and acquired its pavilion in 1903. The town's football club belongs to the same period, but it seems to have not flourished as much as its rival at Builth Road, and other clubs, like Builth Wednesday and Builth Rangers, waxed and waned. The Golf Club was founded in 1923 beside the Chwefri on the western outskirts of the town. In 1922, through the generosity of Thomas Lant, land adjoining the Groe was opened as a recreation ground for the town, with a pavilion and restaurant, a bowling green and tennis courts.

No large hotels were built to accommodate the town's visitors, though the Lion was enlarged and offered the services of an horse-drawn omnibus which

The Wye in flood

Builth cricket team

met all the trains. The Lion was certainly the largest and most handsome hotel in the town, Georgian, three-storied, and stone-built, its five-bayed frontage with large sash windows, central porch, and cast-iron balustrade, suggests what Builth might have achieved. But the Lion's pretensions were modest enough, describing itself as 'family and commercial'. At the Queen's

LION HOTEL,

BROAD STREET, BUILTH WELLS.

JOHN DAVIES,

PROPRIETOR.

This Hotel is replete with every accommodation for visitors is within a short distance of the Mid-Wales Railway Station and an Omnibus meets every train.

POSTING IN ALL ITS BRANCHES.

LONDON AND DUBLIN PORTER STORES.

Wine and Spirit Merchant.

The Lion Hotel, 'replete with every accommodation for visitors'

Head, now gone, Mrs Price offered 'cigars and well-aired beds', and in Garth Road the three-storied Greyhound, which had been rebuilt in stone under slate with an elegant cast-iron balustrade running the length of its front, prided itself in its home-brewed ales and good stabling. The Swan in West Street was also rebuilt in stone and brick under a mansard roof, with a touch of the architectural panache favoured at the time. The tympanum above the front door was filled with a colourful, three-dimensional representation of a swan. For those of a more sober temperament there was the Temperance Family & Commercial Hotel which, though in Station Road, claimed with blatant inaccuracy it was near the wells.

Boarding-houses abounded and were, on the whole, preferred to hotels. The Glyngwy in the Groe, under the care of Mrs Morgan, the proprietress,

LLANELWEDD VILLA, BUILTH WELLS.

Within 150 yards of Builth Station. Good accommodation for Visitors and Tourists, also Commercials. Stands within its own grounds. Two Reception Rooms, Front Parlour and Drawing-Room, Six Bedrooms, Bathroom, hot and cold, and W.C. Splendid view of the River Wye, and the hills and rocks surrounding it. Two to three miles of good trout fishing free to visitors staying at the Villa. Croquet grounds and ornamental shrubbery. Charges moderate. Good stabling and lock-up coach house. T. LEWIS, Proprietor.

Builth's visitors preferred boarding-houses to hotels

BUILTH WELLS.

Superior Accommodation. Board and Private Sitting-Rooms, with the conveniences and substantial comforts of a home. Well-ventilated Bedrooms, Bathroom, Lavatory, &c.

The house stands in its own grounds, and is situated most picturesquely, adjoining the People's Park and River Wye. Commands beautiful and extensive views from all the rooms. Near Church, Railway Station, and Post Office; also within easy distance of the celebrated Mineral Waters—Saline, Sulphur, and Chalybeate.

Terms moderate. Apply to Mrs. POWELL, Brynhyfryd.

TENNIS AND CROQUET GROUND. BOATING ON THE WYE.

What was offered by landladies and guest-houses was very limited by modern standards

offered: 'Private appartments overlooking the Wye and the Groe Green, charming surroundings, a bathroom, and perfect sanitation.' There were cafés, too, like the Market Coffee Tavern, which was also a boarding-house, and Mr Isaac Davies of Bristol House offered 'hot & cold dinners on Market and Fair Days at moderate prices'. Another establishment at the back of the High Street overlooking the Groe had painted on its wall (still to be seen) that it not only offered its visitors a diningroom, but also hot and cold baths.

In the names of its houses and shops the town clearly saw itself as a place of fashion, abreast of the rest of the country. There was a Cavendish House, a London House, a Bristol House, a Manchester House, and a Crystal House,

The names of local shops were intended to give Builth a cosmopolitan air

with its 'fashionable selection of shawls, mantles, millinery, silk & fancy dresses'. Likewise Gilbert Eadie, who with his sons made and sold boots and shoes in the High Street, assured his patrons, wherever they came from, that his 'homemade waterproof Shooting Boots are worn by all the leading gentry'. Some of Builth's shopkeepers showed impressive versatility. L.J. Jenkins and Son, owners of the Corner Shop in the High Street, could not only provide 'suits made to measure at the shortest notice, fit & style guaranteed', but also offered a hearse and pair for hire.

Shops acquired new frontages, and happily one of these has survived in the chemist's shop, No. 11 High Street. Its ornate cast-iron pillars and window surrounds must have had many counterparts along the street in their day. As trade grew, some houses were converted into shops. One of these was Wye House on the corner of Broad Street and Bridge Street. Built in the 1860s it is said to have been the first house in the town to install a complete water system, even able to provide its occupants with hot baths. It was the home of Evan T. Owen, a solicitor prominent in local affairs as Clerk to the Board of Guardians and the Local Government Board. By 1918 part of its ground floor had been given over to a shop and offices.

Visitors were assured they kept the very best of company when they shopped at Builth

Mr Eadie's 'waterproof shooting boots were worn by the leading gentry'

At heart, Builth was always a market town, and the saddler and harness maker prospered

1901, the end of an era: Builth mourns the
death of Queen Victoria

Builth's career as a spa town ended with the First World War. Most of its patrons came from South Wales, where the depression of the 1920s was deeper and more prolonged than was often the case elsewhere, and the expense of holidays could now not easily be met. A spa cure could last three weeks or longer, which was beyond the length of the average working man's holiday. Consequently spas of somewhat moderate calibre, such as Builth, had to compete with the growing popularity of seaside resorts on the basis of their amenities alone. To compensate for this decline Builth developed its role as a market town, while still offering inland holiday facilities such as fishing and, more recently, pony trekking. But even as late as 1938 the urban district council debated the wisdom of mounting a campaign to advertise the town as a health resort.

CHAPTER TWO

Health, Law and Order

A ccording to early guidebooks, Builth had 'long been valued for the salubrity of its air and the singular beauty of its position upon the banks of the finest river in South Wales'. No one would dispute the latter part of this claim, but when in November 1854 the town's Baptist minister died of cholera, the salubrity of Builth's air seemed very much a matter of doubt.

The antiquary Benjamin Malkin (1769–1842) visited Builth in 1803. He entered the town from the Brecon road: 'The entrance to the town is at the upper of two parallel streets; built by a singular arrangement in rude terraces on the side of a steep declivity. This upper street is clean and comfortable . . . but the lower and most populous street is as fashionless, as miserable, as dirty as anything I have hitherto witnessed.' If this is a tolerant judgement on the condition of Builth in the early nineteenth century, the inadequacy of its

Sheep fairs in Market Street contributed little to the town's hygiene

In 1866 Bank Square was drained with open sewers. Again sheep sales did not help

sanitary arrangements needs no emphasis. It was all a matter of gravitation. Waste, rubbish and sewage all flowed into the lower parts of the town and the river. The problem was compounded by the amount of animal manure in the streets.

As a first step towards alleviating this situation, Builth Local Board built a culvert over the Lampercilly Brook to the Groe in June 1840. This small brook ran down Smithfield Road, and from its junction in West Street ran directly to Llanfair House, across Groe Green and into the Wye. In 1843 it was proposed to spend £54 on repairing and making new sewers in the town to relieve the 'effects of filth and bad drainage'. At the same time the scavengers had their wages increased to 7s. a week.

Outside privies were a major nuisance and the town's Nuisance Committee addressed itself to the problem in August 1865. In other parts of the town dunghills, placed in front of houses, were a problem. Then in 1866, in consequence of the Public Health Act, a local board of health was formed at Builth. One of its duties was to appoint a sanitary inspector and one of its first tasks was to improve the town's water and sewerage arrangements. Hitherto Builth was supplied with water by wells and some twenty or so private pumps. Mr Timothy Curley of Hereford, a chartered engineer, was

The opening of the new water reservoir, 1897

consulted, and paid £50 for a survey from which he concluded: 'I must say I have never inspected any town that requires sanitary works more than Builth.'

Under the supervision of Timothy Curley a sewerage and waterworks scheme was constructed in 1867/8. It was further improved in 1897 when its reservoirs and waterworks were established 600 ft above sea level, just west of the Brecon Road, and the whole enterprise cost just over £3,000. The opening of the gas works in 1865 meant that street lighting could also now be provided. The medical advantages of these improvements were not, however, immediately apparent. The problem was one of education. In 1846 the vicar commented upon the dirtiness of some of his parishioners: 'I found a house in Builth where the bedroom was downstairs. I found two pigs in one corner and children ill with scarlet fever in the other.' In 1867 diarrhoea, typhus, typhoid fever and measles broke out in the town. One of the town's doctors, Thomas Jones, caught typhus from a pauper patient. Thirty-three years later, in December 1900, a diphtheria epidemic closed the schools. Then in October 1902 there was an outbreak of scarlet fever, followed by whooping cough in December. In October 1903 measles again closed the schools. Mumps were a scourge in 1909, followed by influenza in 1910.

In the 1860s and 1870s the town was served by two doctors, Dr Jones and Dr Bennet. The level of contemporary medical knowledge is illustrated in

Mr W.E. Dixon, plumber and sanitary engineer, needed a large staff to improve the town's arrangements

Kilvert's grim account of the Llysdinam waggoner who, in May 1871, was suffering from meningitis. Dr Bennet, a Member of the Royal College of Surgeons of England and a Licentiate of the Society of Apothecaries, 'was attending, shaving his head, bleeding, leeching, blistering, fomenting with gin, vinegar, and water on the forehead, hot bottles to the feet, mustard plaisters to the calves of the legs and ice for the forehead'. The ice was obtained from a Hereford fishmonger by train. It left Hereford at 3.40 p.m., arriving at Three Cocks at 4.45 p.m. From here a train left for Builth at 5.37 p.m., delivering the ice for Dr Bennet's patient at 6.15 p.m. exactly.

In 1881 Llandrindod Hospital opened. Its facilities were available to patients from Builth, though this was not a very convenient arrangement. It prevailed until 1896, when, as part of the town's celebration of Queen Victoria's Diamond Jubilee, the Builth Cottage Hospital and Convalescent Home was constructed. It had been the long-held desire of Mr John Davies of Wye Terrace that the town should have its own hospital. He died, however,

Staff and patients at the Cottage Hospital

before his wish was fulfilled, but he left a large sum of money to his sisters-in-law, Miss Margaret and Miss Elizabeth Powell, who set aside £6,000 to build and endow a hospital which opened on 27 October 1897 with six beds and room for a further six. Other monies, from donations, subscriptions, and fund-raising, were added to the endowment fund. A list of subscribers can be seen on a brass plaque in the hospital's hallway. The building itself cost £2,738. By the end of its first year it had admitted twenty-nine patients and by 1899 this number had risen to forty-three.

In 1912 patients living within the area covered by the Builth Poor Law Union paid 2s. 6d. a week while staying in the hospital, and those outside the union paid 5s. Private patients were also accepted and their terms were fixed by negotiation with the Hospital Committee. During the First World War soldiers came to the hospital to convalesce, and after the war a grateful town contributed towards providing it with an operating theatre as part of its war memorial. Other improvements and extensions followed.

Dentistry made similar progress. Travelling dentists attended on fair days, relying more on speed and strength rather than anaesthetics. But in 1881 Mr Sellis, who advertised himself in the local paper as a surgeon dentist and used the initials RCS (but made no claim to the college's licenciate in dentistry) offered his patients the prospect of painless operations and dentures which required neither wires nor springs to keep them in place. He claimed they could be fitted without the previous extraction of dental stumps, and he

First World War soldiers being driven from Builth station to convalesce at the Cottage Hospital

could be consulted on Mondays in West Street. By the turn of the century the town had two resident dental surgeons, Mr Stewart in High Street, and Mr Holland in West Street. Watch-makers and chemists had sidelines as opticians, and grocers, like Mr Price who had extensive premises in High Street, augmented the services of local pharmacists with patent medicines of guaranteed superior quality.

Builth was slow in acquiring a workhouse. Charities like that of Margaret Powell, who in 1715 bequeathed £20 due to her on the mortgage of a tenement called Hengwm to the poor of the parish, eased the distress of the poor to some measure. The 1834 Poor Law Amendment Act, however, attempted to put relief on a more systematic basis by establishing Boards of Guardians of the Poor, and the Builth Poor Law Union came into existence in January 1837. Consisting of thirty-one parishes and townships, it was superintended by thirty-five guardians. Builth's guardians of the poor preferred 'outdoor relief', and it was not until 1877 that the workhouse, called in a flush of patriotism Victoria House, was erected beyond Victoria Terrace in Victoria Road. It was demolished in 1941, though the poor law system was not finally abolished until 1948.

Membership of a friendly society offered some protection against hard times and what was often seen as the ignominy of parish relief. One of these societies was the King's Head Friendly Society, which was established in 1834

Victoria House, the workhouse

The Royal Ancient Order of Buffaloes

and met at the now demolished King's Head. In 1859 one of its members was killed by an engine at Rhymney Iron Works and his brother received £10 12s. 6d. from the society, which was wound up in 1862. Other societies represented in the town were the Buffaloes, Odd Fellows, Forresters and Freemasons, who offered their members social activities, as well as support.

Urban district councillors await the arrival of King George V and Queen Mary at Builth Road
Station, 1920

In 1869 a royal commission laid down a number of requirements 'necessary
for civilized social life'. These included a good water supply, a proper drainage
system, the prevention and removal of nuisances, healthy houses in healthy
streets, the inspection of food, proper provision for burial, and the suppression
of the causes of disease. The provision of these necessities was the
responsibility of local government boards, one of which was established in
Builth in 1871. By the Public Health Act of 1872 the local boards were
incorporated into urban sanitary authorities, which in 1894 became urban
and rural district councils. With the emergence of Builth Urban District
Council in 1894 the town's pattern of local government was established until
its abolition in 1974, when in the reorganization of local government it
disappeared, along with the county of Brecon.

With its narrow streets and persistent taste for timber-framed buildings,
concealed behind stone façades, fire was a constant hazard in Builth. Bearing
in mind the urban district council's inherited responsibility for protecting
'civilized social life', it is surprising that in 1897 it disbanded the town's fire
brigade. Consequently, when a serious fire broke out on the premises of

Builth in the 1870s, depicted with wide streets and elegant buildings

The reality was somewhat different. Broad Street before rebuilding

The Crown Hotel survived the 1907 fire
but has now made way for a bank

Woods in Broad Street in August 1907, there was no brigade at hand. Help was sought from brigades at Llandrindod, Hay on Wye and Brecon; the fire, meanwhile, was fought with buckets of water carried in a human chain from the Wye. The Llandrindod brigade, it is related, set out at eight minutes past six, thirteen minutes after the summons for help had been received. But with two requisitioned horses and another one acquired en route, it took over an hour to get to Builth, seven miles away. It needed three hours to get the fire under control, and the damage it caused was estimated at £5,000. Five shops were eventually destroyed and several other premises severely damaged. At one time it was feared that the whole of High Street and Broad Street would be enveloped.

Afterwards, someone had the initiative to produce postcards depicting the fire in lurid detail. The town acquired its first fire engine, which had to be towed by a lorry, in May 1910, and the fire station was established in Smithfield Road. In October 1928 another fire, this time in the High Street, destroyed what was formerly the Flag and Castle Inn. A brick-built shop now stands in its place, with a second-floor bow-shaped oriel window. Another fire victim was the Lamb Hotel, which was gutted in December 1936 and had to be demolished before it could be rebuilt. A public then grateful to its

Builth Wells Urban District fire engine, used from 1910 to 1941

The fire engine was hauled by a steam lorry

fire brigade subscribed £40 to equip it with nine new uniforms. In 1941, when enemy air raids were not inconceivable, Builth acquired its first self-propelling fire engine to replace its ancient 1910 predecessor. Finally, in 1948, Brecon and Radnor Joint Fire Brigade established its headquarters in Builth.

POLICING THE TOWN

Law and order was largely in the hands of justices of the peace who, appointed by the Crown, were drawn from the ranks of the local gentry. They met at Quarter Sessions in Brecon, where Great Sessions were also held. (These were the Welsh equivalent to English Assizes.) A magistrates' room was erected at Builth in 1832, wherein the justices could discuss and settle local affairs. There was also a lock-up for those awaiting judgement or transfer to the county gaol at Brecon. The decision in 1853 of a Builth woman, whose watch had been stolen, to pay a gipsy to bewitch the thief and recover the watch, was as much a reflection of her lack of confidence in the constable as it was of her faith in magic.

When paid county constabularies were first established by Peel's County Police Act of 1839, Breconshire took no advantage of the act and in 1847 the vicar and Mr Thomas of Welfield were moved to provide constables at their own expense, to assist the town's solitary policeman. It was not until 1856

The fairs were times of hiring labour and drunkenness

that Breconshire joined with its Radnorshire neighbour to establish a police force. This decision was forced upon the still reluctant two counties by the County and Borough Police Act, and by 1857 Builth had a superintendant constable, the cost of whose salary was shared with Radnorshire. He was Jeremiah Rattigan, who came to Builth with some experience in the Irish constabulary and the forces of Cardiganshire and Denbighshire. He stayed in the town for some six years.

It was at this time that the neat stone police station was built in Castle Street. Besides a charge room and cells, there was a court room upstairs, shared by the magistrates for their petty sessions and the judge for the business of the county court. In 1900 petty sessions met on the second and fourth Mondays of the month, and the county court, a means of administering justice established in its present form in 1846, met monthly, occasionally using the Assembly Rooms above the Market Hall instead of the police station. The petty sessions for the Colwyn division of Radnorshire also met at Builth from 1884. These courts, however, no longer meet in Builth and the police station has moved to new buildings in West Street, at the other end of the town. The old police station is now the office of the Registrar of Births, Deaths and Marriages.

The brewery

The offence above all others which brought inhabitants of Builth to the magistrates court was drunkenness. In 1846 the vicar, the Revd Richard Hopkins Harrison (1805–79), complained that there was both a lack of chastity and of what he described as 'delicacy between the sexes' among his flock, but the real problem was drunkenness, which in his opinion was 'the besetting sin of this town to an extent rarely equalled by a very few, if any other parishes in Wales'. The vicar also found his Welsh parishioners more deceitful and less reliable than their English counterparts, and with more of a disposition to pilfer, though 'we are less apprehensive of robbery than in England'. Educated at Trinity College, Oxford, the Revd Richard Harrison came to Builth in 1844 and, despite all his strictures upon his parishioners, cannot have found the living totally unacceptable, for he stayed at Builth until his death in 1879.

CHAPTER THREE

The Inner Man: Religion and Education

The Normans saw the church as much as the castle as a means of conquest and subjugation, and the foundation of the parish church of Builth belongs to the same period as the castle. It is dedicated, as the town's Welsh name (Llanfair ym Muallt) suggests, to Our Lady, a favourite Norman dedication. Nothing more than the dedication has survived of the Norman church, however. It was rebuilt in the late-twelfth or early thirteenth century, and the tower of the original church serves the present building. Its style is functional and defensive rather than ornamental, and its architecture may well have been connected with the castle. Its base is slightly splayed, its windows are no more than small lancets, and it has a battlemented crest. Its

The old white-washed parish church before rebuilding

unbuttressed, military style is a reminder that in troubled times the parish church was often the poor man's castle.

By the 1870s a larger church was needed to accommodate the growing number of summer visitors, and to reflect the aspirations of the town as an inland resort. John Norton (1823–1904) was chosen as the architect, and he has the distinction of being the only architect of national significance to have contributed to Builth. He had a distinguished architectural pedigree, for he was a spiritual grandson of Augustus Welby Northmore Pugin (1812–52), whose *True Principles of Pointed or Christian Architecture* (1841) was a major influence in Gothic Revival. Norton himself was trained by Pugin's pupil, Benjamin Ferry. He also had some fame as a railway architect, and his South Western Hotel of 1872 at Southampton rather overshadows the nearby station.

In the event, Norton's design for Builth church, in the correct Middle Pointed style so esteemed at the time, was not fully implemented, for it involved building a new nave with aisles on both the north and south sides, as well as a new chancel. No doubt because of the cost, the north aisle was omitted and its place was taken by an organ chamber.

The new church had an appearance of romantic complexity, with its varied rooflines and two-storied porch with a turret surmounted by a conical roof cap containing the staircase. The roofs were tiled and patterned, and the tracery of the larger windows was in the decorated style. The four lights of the geometrically designed window at the east end of the chancel were filled with glass by the Pre-Raphaelite stained-glass artist C.E. Kempe. So that public worship could continue while the new church was being built, the nave of 1793 remained in use.

The new church had seats for 450 and cost £3,700, of which Thomas Thomas of Pencerrig gave £1,000. The rest came mainly from public subscription. The new building was consecrated by the Bishop of St Davids on Tuesday 13 July 1875, and such was the approval given to Norton's new church that he was invited to restore nearby Llanelwedd, which he did in 1877.

Today the church is set in a spacious graveyard, which until recently was shaded by rows of trees. They, and the thoroughfares which crossed it, were thought by a visitor to the town early this century to 'give an almost collegiate atmosphere to the quarter'. This atmosphere of collegiate calm was disturbed more than once in the middle of the eighteenth century.

In 1742 the rector of Maesmynis, Edward Phillips, invited John Wesley to visit Builth. Phillips was a Methodist sympathizer and friend of the Wesleys. Though his registers show he was a diligent parish priest he did not live among his parishioners at Maesmynis but in Builth, two miles away, where he

A contemporary print of the rebuilt parish church, 1875

The tree-lined churchyard in which Wesley preached

had taken a house. There was, in fact, no vicarage at Maesmynis at that time and the same had been true of Builth for more than a century when the vicar, the Revd Richard Harrison, came to the town in 1845. He remained its parish priest for some thirty-five years, and had to provide his own vicarage.

But to return to Edward Phillips and the Wesleys. He was a local man, born at Llanfaredd. Two years after graduating at Jesus College, Oxford, he was presented to the living of Maesmynis in 1740. The invitation to John Wesley was probably conveyed, even prompted, by Marmaduke Gwynne, the squire of Garth and the largest landowner in the Hundred of Builth, whose daughter Sarah was to marry Charles Wesley in April 1749. John Wesley performed the ceremony at Llanlleonfel church, noting in his diary: 'I married my brother and Sarah Gwynne. It was a solemn day, such as became the dignity of a Christian marriage.' Charles Wesley fills in the details in his diary:

Not a cloud was to be seen from morning till night. I rose at four; spent three hours and a half in prayer or singing with my brother, with Sally, with Beck [Sally's sister]. At eight I led my Sally to church. Her father, sisters, Lady Rudd, Grace Bowen, Betty Williams and, I think, Billy Tucker and Mr James were all the persons present. . . . We walked back to the house and joined again in prayer. Prayer and thanksgiving was our whole employment. We were cheerful without mirth, serious without

41

John Wesley

sadness. A stranger, that intermeddleth not with our joy, said 'It looked more like a funeral than a wedding'. My brother seemed the happiest person among us.

The visit to Edward Phillips did not, in fact, take place until May 1743; the two men immediately took to each other and Howell Harris told Wesley it had proved a great blessing 'to young Mr Phillips'. Wesley preached in the churchyard at Builth, and not in the church. The frequently read stricture that this was because the incumbent, the Revd Thomas Davies, probably had little time for wandering clerics, may be unjustified. The size of congregation attracted by John Wesley's preaching would have had little prospect of being accommodated in Builth's little church.

It was an impressive occasion. Wesley stood on a tombstone at the east end of the churchyard and preached twice, at four o'clock in the afternoon and at seven in the evening. He was listened to with rapt attention, which is not surprising perhaps, for justices of the peace stood on either side of him – Marmaduke Gwynne and Marmaduke Protheroe – both of whom had come under the influence of the evangelical movement of the day.

In August 1748, when both Charles Wesley and Howell Harris were published to preach in Builth at the same hour, there was something of a contretemps. Charles declared that since it was his intention to preach on that occasion he wondered whether there was any point in Harris doing so as well. Howell Harris, however, replied that since his intention to preach that day had been published a month ago, some of his audience had travelled twenty miles to hear him. Moreover, hundreds of Welshmen would be present who could not follow an English sermon. Charles thereupon gave way.

The eighteenth century, through the influence of the Methodists, also saw the revival of hymn-singing and Charles Wesley is remembered, of course, as a highly talented and indefatigable hymn-writer. The authorship of over five thousand works is ascribed to him. One of these, the controversial 'Jesu, lover of my soul' was written to console the last hours of his wife's old nurse at Llanelwedd.

Another friend of Edward Phillips was Thomas Pritchard. Born in Builth, he became a successful London merchant and when he died in 1756, besides leaving his 'worthy friend' Edward Phillips £300, he bequeathed a further £1,800 in South Sea annuities to charitable purposes in his native town. Litigation ensued and in 1760 it was decreed that there should be: '. . . laid out in building a school-house, paying a salary to the master, placing out the children apprentice, &c., but no house has been built in pursuance of this decree.' The interest was spent, however, in fulfilling two of Thomas Pritchard's intentions: apprenticing children in the town and supporting the poor.

In 1813 the *Cambrian Traveller's Guide* noted: 'There are no less than 4 meeting houses in this small place, the population of which in 1801 was 677 inhabitants and the number of houses was 108. These are crowded every Sunday, and on other days of the week. The first is for the Presbyterians, the second for Baptists, the third for Calvinistic Methodists, and the fourth for Wesleyans.' These chapels have all been rebuilt since 1813, and by some historical accident a Nonconformist chapel now stands at each of the four corners of the churchyard.

The oldest of these congregations seems to be that of the Alpha Presbyterian chapel. The first chapel was built in 1747 under the direction of Howell Harris, who gave his 'New Room' in Builth the name Alpha. Some think it was the first Welsh Methodist chapel. On establishing it, Harris commented, with sad cynicism, that 'God had never before been in Llanfair'. It was rebuilt in 1824 and 1878, and then in 1903 by Habershon, Fawkner, & Groves for £5,400. Now it is a listed building.

Then, it seems, came the Baptists. In 1787 a church of thirteen members started at Noyadd Farm, Llandewi'r Cwm, with the Revd William Jones of Penrheol as its minister. Numbers grew and in 1790 Ebenezer chapel was

Alpha Presbyterian chapel, rebuilt 1903

built in Market Street, opposite The Plough. Ebenezer means 'stone or rock of help' and reflects the light in which many Nonconformists saw their religion at this time. It was indeed seen by many as a rock of help in facing the disapproval of the Establishment, and in dealing with the disadvantages of being a Nonconformist. The chapel was rebuilt in 1816 and 1842, and in 1899 the congregation moved into the present building, complete with spire, in West Street. It was called the Baptist Memorial chapel to commemorate the 80th birthday of Queen Victoria, and was the work of George Morgan & Son of Carmarthen. The original chapel survived until 1989, when it was demolished.

Horeb was originally a Congregational chapel, founded by the Revd David Williams of Beiliheulog. It was built in 1808 and enlarged in 1829. The present building, which also has a spire, was built in 1869 at the cost of £1,800 by R. Moffat Smith, 'the Manchester architect'. He chose a Romanesque style, because Nonconformity was anxious not to be confused architecturally with the Gothic of the Church of England in Wales, though he did allow the extravagance of a small spire capped with a weathercock.

CONGREGATIONAL CHAPEL, BUILTH WELLS BRECONSHIRE.

R. MOFFAT SMITH, ARCHITECT, MANCHESTER.

Congregational chapel of 1869

This no doubt gave Horeb's congregation singular pleasure, for when a Builth guidebook was published by a London publisher in 1869, its view of the town from the Llandrindod Road depicted Horeb's spire rising far higher than the squat tower of the nearby Anglican church. Horeb means 'the desert', and those who established this independent congregation in Builth thought that they had caused the rose of true religion to flourish in the desert of Anglicanism. The chapel was renovated in 1905 and became part of the United Reformed Church in 1972.

The original chapel of the Wesleyan Methodists was erected in 1804 on the corner of Hay and Castle Roads. It was restored in 1866 and served its congregation until 1895, when it acquired its present building in Garth Road. There was no risk, now, of confusion with the Gothic Anglicans, and Wesleyan Methodism was sufficiently self-confident to build a chapel in semi-Gothic style for £1,300. The original chapel was converted into two dwellings, which still exist.

SCHOOLS AND RULES

A continuous tradition of education began at Builth with the foundation of the National School in around 1830. The National Society was formed in 1811 with the aim of establishing elementary schools for the education of the poor, according to the principles of the Church of England. Its school in Builth, often referred to as the 'Endowed School', was built with a schoolroom which, in 1846, inspectors thought to be 'large, light, and airy', on a site near the present primary school. It was closely connected with the parish church. Indeed, most of its pupils also attended the Sunday School which for the boys was held in the same building, and for the girls in the chancel of the parish church. Since there were forty-five female pupils, taught by the vicar's wife and three other ladies of the parish, and the chancel was small, they seemed 'inconveniently huddled together'. In all there were at this time five Sunday schools in the town. A hundred boys and girls attended that of the Anglicans, and 230 the other four denominational Sunday Schools. Nonconformist Sunday Schools often attracted adult pupils, so that, for example, in adjoining Radnorshire where there were twenty-eight Nonconformist schools in 1846, a quarter of the pupils are recorded as being *above* the age of fifteen.

The Rebecca and Chartist riots in Wales during the second quarter of the nineteenth century led the government to set up an inquiry into their cause, which was largely ascribed to a lack of education and the absence of schools. On the motion of William Williams, MP for Coventry, a leading radical of his day, a royal commission was set up to inquire into the state of education in

Wales, 'especially into the means afforded to the labouring classes of acquiring a knowledge of the English language'. Three well-intentioned Anglican lawyers who knew little about Wales, and less Welsh, conducted the inquiry. They met in Builth to examine the local schools in October 1846, staying at the Lion Hotel.

They published their findings in 1847 in three blue-bound volumes, *The Blue Books*, and blamed Nonconformity and the Welsh language for the sorry state of affairs, educationally, morally, and socially, which prevailed among the Welsh nation. Their findings were received with anger and resentment by Anglicans and Nonconformists alike, though they let Builth off rather lightly. The pupils of the National School were considered to be 'very defective and limited in general knowledge', though 'attendance was rather large for a town of this size'. The school, they noted, had been closed for three months before the arrival of Mr Thomas, the present master, whom they thought to be a teacher 'of much promise'. His predecessor had been dismissed for drunkenness.

In January 1879 the infants' department of the National School was separated from the main school, and in April 1896 it moved again to the former Wesleyan chapel at the junction of Castle and Hay Roads. At the same time two rooms were added to the main school, its headmaster noting that many children were hired in the May Hiring Fair; some half-dozen names were removed from the school register. In 1911 a new, two-storeyed school was built in Park Road to replace the nearby endowed school building, by now hopelessly outgrown.

In 1846 a Mr Thomas Grocock and a Mr John Jones both ran private schools in the town. To do so was neither profitable, nor rewarding. John Jones informed the commissioners: 'My terms are twelve shillings per quarter for day scholars. The parents do not know what education means, they think half a year enough to learn everything and take their children away in general, after this time. They can not bear the idea of paying for a book. The parents bargain with the master and beat down his charges. Masters by this means are impoverished and think it better to be almost anything rather than a schoolmaster.'

Until the foundation of Builth County School in 1896, boys who wanted the benefits of secondary education had to seek it at Brecon. A Free Grammar School was attached to the Collegiate Church at Brecon. Of this, the Charity Commissioners remarked in 1836 that, despite its name, 'it does not appear to have been at anytime conducted purely as a free grammar school, the scholars being required to pay between £2 2s. 0d. and £4 4s. 0d. per annum, with the exception of three who were placed upon the foundation and paid the moiety of the sum demanded from the others.' A

Children in the playground of the new National School, built in 1911

new schoolroom was built in 1808 to accommodate 80 boys, but in 1836 the school had only 7 scholars whose ages varied between 6 and 14. Its decline continued and in 1853 it was reconstituted and re-established as a fee-paying public school and an alternative to Llandovery College, founded five years earlier.

There was even less provision for girls, though at the end of the century the town had at least two private academies for the education of young ladies: Miss Florence Morris and her sister Miss Caroline Morris conducted their Young Ladies' School at Wye View House; and at Park House in Park Road Miss Kettle presided over her Ladies College as principal.

Builth County School was one of more than ninety County Schools which came into existence in consequence of the Welsh Intermediate Education Act of 1889. In August 1890 the great Liberal educationist, A.J. Mundella, attended a conference in Builth, for which special excursion trains were laid on from Brecon. At a further meeting in December it was proposed that an Intermediate School should be established in the town for 50 boys and 30 girls. The new Breconshire County Council agreed to provide £448 towards the cost of the school building, on condition that £1,152 and a two-acre site were provided by local voluntary effort.

In 1892, £8,000 was bequeathed by the widow of Evan J. Evans, once professor of Hebrew at New College, London, who had been born at Erwneuadd Farm, Garth. It was intended to provide scholarships for the sons of farmers to attend the new school, which opened on 17 February 1896 in temporary premises. Only 5 pupils attended on the first day, but by the end of the summer term 27 were in attendance. Some of these had to board in the town and the school's *Rules for Licensed Houses* required them to be indoors by 7 p.m. in winter and 8.30 p.m. in summer.

The school was established in its permanent building on 6 May 1889. It was designed by S.W. Williams, the Radnorshire architect and county surveyor, and had accommodation for some eighty pupils. It cost £3,906 to build and equip and much of this was the result of local generosity, Miss Clara Thomas of Llwynmadoc giving £400. The staff at this time consisted of the headmaster and two assistants. Cookery was introduced into the curriculum in 1899, physical science in 1902, woodwork 1906, gardening and agriculture in 1912, and botany and physics in 1916.

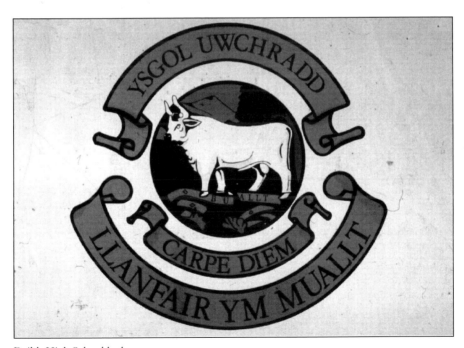

Builth High School badge

However, despite this broadening of the curriculum, in 1906 the school had only 44 pupils on the roll. But by 1914 it was firmly established with a roll of 70 pupils and a staff of 4, most of the pupils staying at the school for 3 years. Numbers now continued to increase with 80 pupils on the roll in 1915, 86 in 1916, 103 in 1917 and 111 in 1918. Consequently the school was becoming overcrowded and more expensive to run; costing £570 in 1896/7, but £941 in 1915/16. An ex-army hut was acquired as a temporary workshop and gymnasium, and some temporary classrooms were provided in 1934. Temporary in Breconshire can be a long time, and it was not until 1960 that the school was given permanent workshops. It was not until 1980 that a permanent gymnasium was acquired! Playing fields were also needed. Meanwhile, the pressure on accommodation was increased by pupils staying until they were 16. Attendance, on the other hand, was often irregular and in 1958 the headmaster complained that some pupils were absent far too often, and that 'sheep-dipping, sheep-shearing, hay and corn harvests' were frequently the cause.

The raising of the school leaving age to 15 in 1947 led to further pressure on accommodation, which was eased with the acquisition of temporary buildings originally used by the Primary School. In 1949 the school became Builth County Secondary School, catering for the education of all local children over the age of 11. There were now 262 pupils on the roll, which by 1956 had grown to 380. In 1977 the school became Builth Wells High School and in 1986/9, S.W. Williams's original building for 80 pupils was enlarged, with handsome extensions of stone and brick under slate, to accommodate over 400 students.

CHAPTER FOUR

Transport, Work and War

OF ROAD AND RAIL

From its earliest days, Builth's importance lay in the crossing of the Wye that it offered, protected by the castle nearby, for those travelling between North and South Wales. Tradition has it that Llewelyn ap Gruffydd destroyed a bridge at Builth in 1282. If this is so, it was not soon replaced, for in 1324 a ferry over the Wye produced for its owners 4s. a year. There followed what was probably a succession of wooden bridges, easier and cheaper to construct than those of stone, and offering less resistance to floodwater and debris. In 1779 a six-arched stone bridge, its piers equipped with strong cut-waters, was built by James Parry of Hay to replace its decaying wooden predecessor. The cost of what is indisputably the most beautiful structure in the town was

Stone commemorating the bridge's reconstructions

Widening Builth bridge in 1925. A single cart occupies its width

The Builth bridge builders of 1925

shared by the counties of Brecon and Radnor, which the bridge linked. In 1791 James Parry built another elegant, though smaller bridge (having but three arches), over the Usk at Aberbran in south Breconshire.

Pride in Builth's new bridge was replaced by anxiety in September 1796, when it seemed in danger of becoming redundant. An advertisement appeared in the *Hereford Journal*: 'As the River Wye is breaking out on the Radnorshire side, and is likely to leave Builth Bridge on dry land, any person, or persons, conversant with Embankments who will, undertake to keep the River in its usual and proper channel are desired to attend, with their Plans and Estimates, at the next General Quarter Sessions of the Peace. . . .'

The bridge was narrow and its parapets rather low; consequently in the panic and confusion which ensued when flocks of animals travelling in opposite directions met on the bridge, there was always the risk that some of them would jump over into the fast-flowing river below. To remove this hazard the parapets were raised to a uniform height of 3ft 9in in 1868. A proposal to ease congestion further by widening the bridge in 1877 came to nothing, and it was not done until 1925.

There was another eighteenth-century bridge, also of stone, but with only three arches, spanning the Irfon and bearing the road westward from Builth to Garth. In 1936 it was replaced by a rather more functional, steel-arched

The eighteenth-century Irfon bridge

The 1936 Irfon bridge under construction

The completed bridge of steel girders

The 1839 suspension bridge over the Irfon

successor. Another bridge, this time an iron suspension bridge, was erected in 1839 over the Irfon for those wanting access to Park Wells. It was, in fact, a second-hand structure, originally built in 1866 over the Usk in Lord Genusk's park near Crickhowel. When in 1868 it was found to be in need of repair, the tender of Robert Lewis, a local carpenter, for £12 8s. 6d. was accepted. It was closed in 1983 and stylishly replaced the following year.

The maintenance of roads was a parochial responsibility, and each vestry appointed its own surveyor of the highway, who was often reluctant to assume office and had to be bribed to do so. The cost of repairs and labour was met by parish rates. The system was not efficient and roads were often impassable for mud and ruts. It was complained that they were 'in divers Places so bad and ruinous, especially in the Winter Season, that Travellers and Carriages cannot pass without great Danger, and the said Roads cannot by ordinary Course be provided by the laws of this Kingdom for repairing the Highways be effectually mended and kept in good Repair, unless some provision be made for raising Money to be applied for that Purpose.' (Kington Turnpike Act, 1756.)

Towards the end of the eighteenth century the maintenance of the main roads in the counties of Brecon and Radnor was taken over by Turnpike Trustees. The trustees were local men of substance, having 'in their own right or in the right of their wives lands of the yearly value of £100 or real or

Milestone on the turnpike road from
Builth to Kington

personal estate worth £2000.' Each trust elected a treasurer, clerk, and
surveyor, and shared the profits from the tolls they charged which remained
after they had repaired the roads in their care.

From 1767 toll houses and turnpike gates across the road became part of
the Breconshire landscape and were set up at Builth on the Hay Road
opposite White House; on the Old Brecon Road opposite the Plough; on the
Garth Road; and over the bridge on the Rhaeadr and Llandrindod Roads,
which forked at the Llanelwedd Arms. Sadly, with the exception of Gate
House on the Llandrindod Road, none of these toll houses has survived. Any
improvement in the roads under the care of Turnpike Trustees seems to have
been slow in becoming apparent. In 1792 Mr Lea, landlord of the then Royal
Oak at Builth, ran a waggon service for freight, and stage coaches for
passengers. In view of the heavy toll he paid at the turnpike gates he expected
the road to Hay to be improved from the bad state into which it had
deteriorated. Consequently, he charged the Turnpike Trust with negligence at
the Quarter Sessions. This was a strategic move on Mr Lea's part, because
several local justices were also Turnpike Trustees.

What the outcome was of this initiative is uncertain, but in the following
January Thomas Jones of Pencerrig, a magistrate, recorded in his account
book that he had received £31 10s. 0d. from the Turnpike Road Trust

towards a new road'. Progress was slow. When, in 1811, the agriculturalist Walter Davies (1761–1849), travelled along the turnpike to Builth from Llandrindod, he complained: 'On the level between Llandrindod and Pencerrig a trough of mud and ruts so deep and the road so narrow that two horses can hardly pass without danger and yet there is a toll and a gate at Builth.'

In fact this road, which was part of the Newtown–Builth turnpike, was not completed and made fit for coaches by being macadamized until 1823. It was built at the cost of £10,000 by the Montgomeryshire radical, William Pugh (1793–1842). Other improvements followed, so that the road from Builth by way of Hundred House, Glascwm, Colva and Gladestry to Kington was described as 'a good turnpike' in 1836. In 1840 it was announced that the post was to be brought that way so that Builth might receive its London letters two hours earlier.

The tolls charged in Breconshire in 1844 were the highest in South Wales: '9d. for a horse drawing a carriage with springs; 6d. for carts and wagons; and 2d. for a horse when ridden'. There were reduced terms for stage coaches because of the number of horses hauling them. Tolls were particularly resented by farmers and drovers who, if they were driving their cattle into Builth, would have 10d. per score to enter the town, and the same amount on their way out. This led them to avoid the town and to use hill tracks over the Eppynt instead. At the same time, the toll gates and their adjoining houses came to be seen by the agricultural poor of the upper Wye Valley as the symbolic cause of their poverty, to be attacked and destroyed. In October 1843 as the riots intensified an officer and twenty men of the 4th Light Dragoons were sent from London and stationed in the town. A more persistent hazard for the turnpike gate-keepers were drunken visitors to the fairs who were reluctant or unable to pay the tolls, a situation exacerbated by the hospitality readily available from the seventeen public houses in the town.

Those who had neither horse nor carriage could travel by stage coach which was, due to the motion, often uncomfortable. If one travelled as an outside passenger it was also dangerous. But for the intrepid traveller, the *Royal Dart* began a daily summer service in 1828 from Newtown to Brecon, via Builth. With improved road surfaces during the 1840s coach services expanded. The *Lily of the Valley* ran from Builth to Cheltenham via Hay on alternate days, and in 1850 the *Mazeppa* ran three times a week from Builth to Hereford, via Hay and Glasbury. One of the last coaches to serve the town was the *Railway Queen*, which in 1861 was running between Knighton and Builth. But the stage coach could not survive the advent of the railway.

Builth eventually acquired three railway stations bearing its name, but they were all on the Radnorshire side of the Wye at a discreet distance from the

The steam engine arrives at Builth, 1864. The Mid-Wales Railway's construction locomotive *Venus*

town, as if it were at first uncertain as to the advantages railways had to offer. The town's railway history began formally with the opening of the Mid-Wales Railway on 23 August 1864, when a special train ran from Brecon and Three Cocks through Builth along the Wye Valley, through Newbridge and Rhaeadr to Llanidloes and back. Regular services commenced a month later with three passenger and two mixed trains running daily each way. It was four years since parliament had passed the necessary legislation. Gradually, a substantial complex of station buildings evolved, there being two signal boxes, a carriage shed, a goods shed, and cattle pens, as well as the actual station building. From 1 May 1865 the Royal Mail went from Builth by rail.

On 1 November 1866 the Central Wales Extension Railway arrived at Builth Road from Llandrindod. Starting at the Craven Arms and travelling through Knighton to Llandrindod and Builth Road, its intention was to continue via Llangammarch and Llanwrtyd to Llandovery. The Central Wales Extension Railway Station was at Builth Road, where the line crossed that of the Mid-Wales Railway. Though it was 2 miles away, it was intended to be a station for the town. The track was single and there was no second platform. Its line on to Garth opened on 11 March 1867 in heavy snow, which did little to deter the local population, anxious to travel to Builth Market for the first time by train. The line to Llandovery opened on 1 June 1868.

In its day the track layout at Builth was extensive

Builth's importance as a railway centre seemed about to increase still further in 1877, when the Worcester and Aberystwyth Junction Railway proposed a terminus at Builth. The scheme, however, came to nothing, but a link was built between the lines of the Mid-Wales and Central Wales Extension Companies at Builth Road, and in 1889 the Mid-Wales Company's station, originally called Llechryd, was renamed Builth Road Low Level. A hydraulic lift had been installed two years earlier to facilitate the transfer of passengers' luggage and other goods between the two stations. By 1893 the Central Wales line through Builth Road had been doubled; a new Up platform had been built and a proper Down station erected, to replace the original modest waiting shed.

The arrival of two railway lines with stations at Builth and Builth Road offered the town welcome opportunities for new employment. The 1881 census returns for Builth included the names of more than thirty railwaymen, most of whom had families, living mainly in Bank Square and Oaklands. At Builth Road a small community of nearly fifty houses grew up, which was as much a railway town, though in miniature, as its much larger counterparts at Swindon and Crewe. Railway Terrace was built opposite the high-level station between 1881 and 1886, and Wye View Terrace, with twenty-five

Railway Terrace, Builth Road

houses, was erected in the early 1890s. A school was built at Cwmbach in 1865 at the expense of the ever-generous Miss Clara Thomas, which had to be enlarged in the 1890s.

Down the road at Builth station the staff comprised of station master, four signalmen, two shunters, a guard, district inspector, two booking-office clerks, three goods porters, a weighbridge man, and a dray driver. Until 1903 the Mid-Wales Railway also had its locomotive, carriage, and wagon shops at Builth, which offered further jobs. All the same, though the coming of the railways offered the town employment, their arrival did not result in any large-scale development.

Day excursionists came to Builth by train in hundreds. In August 1869, two special trains from Merthyr Tydfil and Dowlais brought a thousand visitors between them. They were members of the Foresters Friendly Society. Some of those who came were distinguished; among them were King George V and Queen Mary, who in July 1920 stayed overnight in the royal train in a siding at Builth Road, on their way to their engagements in Breconshire.

In its heyday, the central Wales line was very busy. In 1911 there were eighteen Up and nineteen Down passenger trains a day. The freight traffic was also heavy and 6,000 tons of anthracite passed through Builth Road High

Wye View Terrace, Builth Road

Level Station weekly, travelling north. In the years between the wars there was a train in each direction between Swansea and Shrewsbury, even boasting the luxury of a restaurant car.

The Central Wales Extension Railway gave way to the London and North Western, which in turn became part of the London, Midland and Scottish in 1922. A different succession of liveries was seen at Builth station; the Mid-Wales Railway being vested in the Cambrian Railways in 1904, which in 1922 became part of the Great Western Railway. Uniformity eventually came with the nationalization of the railways in 1948.

The Second World War had seen a temporary upsurge of railway traffic, but from 1950 onwards decline set in. Petrol was no longer rationed and there was a growth in car ownership. One of the first garages in the town was at the Lion Hotel. Bus services had also been developing. Between the wars Crossville Motors established a Builth–Llandrindod service, which was augmented by Sergeants' service from Kington and Jones' buses linking Builth and Llanwrtyd. Since the end of the Second World War Brown's coaches have served the area.

.On 30 November 1962 the line from Brecon to Moat Lane was closed. The staff at Builth station were transferred to Builth Road, and work began on taking up the track and demolishing the station buildings. The ultimate

61

The death knell of the railway was sounded by the car. The Lion Garage in the 1930s

An early motor car with a visitor from Swansea outside the Lion Hotel

triumph of the internal combustion engine over the steam engine is symbolized locally by the roundabout, which now covers the site of the level crossing at Builth where for ninety-eight years road traffic had to give way to rail. The Central Wales line, on the other hand, remained, and there is still a station at Builth Road, through which the last steam-hauled passenger train ran on 13 June 1964. It was the 6.25 p.m. Swansea–York mail, hauled by a Class 5 4-6-0 locomotive, No. 45406.

COMMERCE AND INDUSTRY

Builth's connection with agriculture, especially cattle and sheep, is as old as its Welsh name, Buellt, deemed to commemorate 'the wild ox of the wooded slope'. In 1324 the value of a cow in Builth was held to be 6s. 8d., and through all the vicissitudes of its long history the town's market flourished. Appropriately a bull is the town's symbol and appears over the entrance of the Market Hall.

Strangely, however, there was no market place; on market days cattle were sold in the High Street, and sheep in Market Street and Bank Square. The result was chaos. In 1903 a visitor noted how Builth had still not 'succeeded in shaking off the time-honoured but inconvenient custom of holding its

Builth's symbolic bull on the Market Hall

A cattle market in the High Street

markets in its main street, which for the most part is some twenty feet wide, and presents on the momentous occasions a scene of indescribable and congested animation. Every vendor of stock is strained to the uttermost to keep his bunch of terrified four-footed wares separate from those of his neighbours. Such a capering and bellowing of Herefords of all ages, such tossing of long horns, such whack, whacking of sticks, such shouting of men and barking of collies never was heard in so cramped a space.'

Even Sundays did not escape this congestion, and in 1869 a man was fined £1 with 8s. 6d. costs for driving a herd of swine through the town on a Sunday. But in 1905 it was decided that enough was enough and a public meeting was held to discuss building a market place. It was three years before plans were drawn up for a cattle market to be established on a site adjacent to Victoria Terrace on the Brecon Road, and two more before the work was completed. Builth's new Smithfield opened in April 1910 and cost £3,400. The cattle and sheep, of course, still had to be taken in droves through the streets to the station, from whence special trains took them to their ultimate destination. Up to 2,500 lambs are still auctioned weekly besides cattle, and during the autumn sheep sales 56,000 lambs and ewes are sold.

By the close of the eighteenth century both Breconshire and Radnorshire had flourishing agricultural societies. Patronized by the gentry, they held

A sheep market at the new Smithfield Market

Horse fair in the late 1940s. Draught horses were still used on the farm

SALMON FISHERY ACT, 1861.

The Committee of the (Builth) Wye Preservation Society beg to call the attention of the Public to the following extracts from the Salmon Fisheries Act, 1861, (24 & 25 Vic., c. 109.)

LAW OF FISHING.

No Person shall do the following things or any of them, that is to say—

(1) Use any Light for the purpose of Catching Salmon;

(2) Use any Spear, Gaff, Strokehall, Snatch, or other like Instrument for Catching Salmon;

(3) Have in his possession a Light, or any of the foregoing Instruments, under such circumstances as to satisfy the Court before whom he is tried that he intended at the time to Catch Salmon by means thereof;

And any Person acting in contravention of this section, shall incur a penalty not exceeding £5, and shall forfeit any Instruments used by him, or found in his possession, in contravention of this section. (sec. 8).

No Person shall do the following things or any of them, that is to say—

(1) Use any Fish Roe for the purpose of Fishing;

(2) Buy, Sell, or expose for Sale, or have in his possession any Salmon Roe;

And any Person acting in contravention of this section shall, for each offence, incur a penalty not exceeding £2, and shall forfeit all Salmon Roe found in his possession. (sec. 9).

No Person shall take, or attempt to take, Salmon with any Net having a Mesh of less dimensions than two inches, in extension from knot to knot, (the measurement to be made on each side of the square) or eight inches measured round each Mesh when wet; and any person acting in contravention of this section shall forfeit all Nets and Tackle used by him in so doing, and shall, for each offence, incur a penalty not exceeding £5; and the placing two or more Nets behind or near to each other in such manner as to practically diminish the Mesh of the Nets used, or the covering the Nets used with canvas, or the using any other artifice so as to evade the provisions of this section with respect to the Mesh of Nets shall be deemed to be an act in contravention of this section. (sec. 10).

No Person shall do any of the following things, that is to say—

(1) Wilfully take any unclean or unseasonable Salmon;

(2) Buy, Sell, or expose for Sale, or have in his possession any unclean or unseasonable Salmon, or any part thereof;

And any Person acting in contravention of this section shall incur the following penalties, that is to say—

(1) He shall forfeit any Fish taken, bought, sold, or exposed for Sale, or in his possession;

(2) He shall incur a penalty not exceeding £5 in respect of each Fish taken, bought, sold, or exposed for sale, or in his possession.

No Person shall do the following things or any of them, that is to say—

(1) Wilfully take or destroy the young of Salmon;

(2) Buy, Sell, or expose for Sale, or have in his possession the young of Salmon;

(3) Place any device for the purpose of obstructing the passage of the young Salmon;

(4) Wilfully injure the young of Salmon;

(5) Wilfully disturb any Spawning Bed, or any Bank or Shallow on which the Spawn of Salmon may be;

And any person acting in contravention of this section shall incur the following penalties, that is to say—

(1) He shall forfeit all the young of Salmon found in his possession;

(2) He shall forfeit all Rods, Lines, Nets, devices, and Instruments used in committing any of the above offences;

(3) He shall for each offence pay a penalty not exceeding £5. (sec. 15).

If any Person wilfully disturbs or attempts to catch Salmon when Spawning, or when on or near their Spawning Beds, he shall for each offence incur a penalty not exceeding £5. (sec. 16).

CLOSE TIME.

No Person shall fish, or catch, or attempt to catch, or kill Salmon between the first day of September and the first day of February following, both inclusive, except only that it shall be lawful to Fish with a Rod and Line between the first day of September and the first day of November following, both inclusive; and any person acting in contravention of this section shall forfeit any Salmon caught by him, and shall in addition thereto incur a penalty not exceeding £5, and a further penalty not exceeding £2 in respect of each Salmon so caught. (sec. 17).

No Person shall buy, sell, or expose for sale, or have in his possession for sale any Salmon between the third day of September, and the second day of February following, and any person acting in contravention of this act shall forfeit any Fish so bought, sold, or exposed for sale, or in his possession for sale, and shall incur a penalty not exceeding £2 for each such Fish. (sec. 19.)

Builth Wye Preservation Society attempted to regulate local fishing monthly meetings of a very convivial nature and encouraged good farming among their tenants and bailiffs by offering premiums for prize stock and crops. In 1833 Builth acquired its own Ploughing and Hedging Society, which encouraged the local improvement of agricultural practice with competitions and prizes. It was followed in 1865 by the Irfon Valley Agricultural Society.

The Wye, of course, has always enjoyed great fame for its fishing. In May 1791 Captain Thomas Jones of Brecon had a 'grand fishing party with nets on the Wye and Irfon', dining afterwards at the Royal Oak. When his friend Thomas Jones of Pencerrig fished in the river in May 1794, he caught seventeen salmon, three large pike, and one shad. This last species was a herring which breeds in freshwater and has become exclusive to the Severn and Wye in Britain. With such tempting prizes, poaching was prevalent and attempts at control were made by the Builth Wye Preservation Society. Its members were landowners whose estates bordered the banks of the Wye. In 1862 their chairman was George Greenwood of Abernant, near Builth, and meetings were held in the Lion Hotel. Encouraged by the Duke of Beaufort they were committed to the 'effectual preservation of the River Wye and its tributaries'. They contributed to the wages of constables and a police sergeant and employed four 'watchers' to augment the landlords' bailiffs. The successful conviction of poachers was rewarded by a guinea, paid to the officer responsible for their detection.

Legitimate salmon fishing was then a pleasure for the privileged few. In April 1875 the Revd Francis Kilvert, the curate of Clyro, travelled by train to Llechryd (as the station at Builth Road was then known), to join a friend fishing:

> . . . presently a fish rose at him, he struck it, and within a quarter of an hour the salmon was gasping on the bank, an 8 lb fish. We crossed the river to him, and there was a consultation whether the salmon was a clean fish. He was not in first rate order, and had probably been in the river some time, but had the 'travelling mark' raw under his throat and so sentence was given that he was a good fish and he was knocked on the head. . . . Soon after we left him Col. Pearson killed another salmon in beautiful order, 11 lbs, and Mr Venables brought it up into my room in triumph to show me, whilst I was dressing for dinner.

Builth was a town of shopkeepers rather than manufacturers. Indeed it was once described as a place where 'the indolent life of trifling behind a counter is generally preferred to the more rational and manly occupation of cultivating and improving the ground'. One reason why no industry developed was the lack of coal. Peat obtained locally was burned for fuel, then 'when their stock of peat proves insufficient, they send to Brecon for coal at the distance of 15 or 20 miles, over bad uneven roads.' This was carried by packhorse or mule and was very expensive. It remained so until the coming of the railways. It is surprising, though, that more use was not made of water power, which was in abundant supply.

The principal exports of the town were butter and cheese, wool and woollen stockings, knitted as a cottage industry, and all were connected with the town's agricultural setting. It was able, however, to supply its own needs, and Thomas Jones in his *Day Book* shows Builth as having an apothecary, attorney, butcher, carpenter, maltster, saddler, shoemaker, tanner, and undertaker. He also records how in 1796 at Pencerrig his two dairymaids made 662 lb of butter, of which 570 lb were sold at Builth at 8d. a pound, the rest being consumed by the household.

In 1865 the Builth Gas and Coke Company built its gasworks and a house for the manager at Oaklands, near the castle site. But by far the largest secular building in the town was the brewery. Stone-built under slate, it was four storeys high with a central six-storeyed hipped-roofed tower. The cattle trade gave rise to a considerable amount of tanning. One tannery was down by the Groe and another is commemorated by such names as Tanhouse Terrace, Tanhouse, and Tanhouse Bridge. The 1883 Ordnance Survey map also records a tannery behind West Street.

Banks were slow in arriving at Builth, perhaps partly because of an innate wariness of bankers in country communities at this time, and partly because drovers, who dealt with large sums of money in their sheep and cattle transactions in the English smithfields, often acted as local bankers. In August 1792 Thomas Jones of Pencerrig lent his brother a Kington bank bill for £10. The Kington bank issuing this note opened in 1789 and was the predecessor of the much more successful Kington and Radnorshire Bank of 1789, which eventually became part of the Midland Bank. The most successful early Welsh bank was the Old Brecon Bank, founded by Wilkins and Co. in 1778 and eventually taken over by Lloyds. The National Provincial Bank of England, now the National Westminster, opened a permanent branch in Builth in 1862, though it had already been offering market-day banking facilities for some years before. The London and Provincial Bank, now Barclays, followed in 1874. By the end of the century Builth also had several drapers, grocers, builders, and a coal merchant, all of which were labour-intensive businesses and employed several assistants. The post office, which until 1936 was in Castle Street, also had a substantial staff of clerks, postmen and telegraph boys by modern standards. In 1918 a Chamber of Trade was founded to develop the town's business interests.

In 1910 Builth post office had a large staff

In 1876 two market halls were built, both in somewhat exotic architectural styles. Yellow brick with stone facings was used by Mr Oliver Morgan Bligh of Cilmeri Park for Strand Hall. He favoured a semi-classical style with a large rose window in the pediment. It could have passed as a large Nonconformist chapel with its side aisles, porch and narthex, and perhaps its intention was to serve as a temple of commerce. The Bligh arms, with the family motto *Finem Respice* (consider the end) enclosed in a medallion, decorate the porch. Bligh also built Glanirfon Terrace in the High Street nearby.

The other hall was built by the Market Hall Company and was designed by the Haddon brothers. As early as 1842 'it had been in contemplation to erect a market house rear of the bridge on a piece of ground belonging to E.D. Thomas of Welfield House'. The building was, though, an unconscionable time in materializing. It eventually opened in November 1877 and is now deemed by some to be the town's best building. The work of the Haddon brothers was already well known because of a 'perverse little Gothic job', Eign Street Congregational church in Hereford, built by them in 1872. Their substantial piece of civic architecture in Builth reflected the self-confidence of the town as a developing spa.

For their Market Hall the Haddon brothers produced an imitation of a thirteenth- or fourteenth-century Italian town hall. It is, in the words of

The chapel-like Strand Hall was built in 1876

The arms of Oliver Morgan Bligh of Cilmeri Park, who built the hall, decorate its entrance

Richard Haslam, 'of stone, with an arcade of seven varied openings below, some with traceries, then terracotta portrait roundels, terracotta machiolations, and a big red-tiled hipped roof'. Upstairs, above the market hall, it housed at one time the offices of the County Court and also had accommodation for public meetings.

Stone was the building material most used in the town, in abundant supply from various local quarries. The most important of these was at Llanelwedd. Early guidebooks mention 'the fantastic and irregular rocks of Llanelwedd' and in June 1796 Thomas Jones of Pencerrig paid £15 for the hauling of a hundred loads of Llanelwedd stone. The Gelli Cadwgan quarry opened at Llanelwedd in 1895. It was developed by Thomas Lant, a Northumbrian who was a great benefactor to Builth. When he won a contract to supply stone for the Elan valley dams that were being built to supply Birmingham with water, a siding was built from the quarry to Builth station, to enable the stone to be sent direct to the Elan valley by rail. At the peak of its activity three hundred men were employed, some of whom were brought in from as far away as Cornwall and Scotland. But once the dams were completed demand for the stone fell, and the quarry closed in 1904.

Territorials on parade outside the Market Hall at the outbreak of war, 1914

A trio of steam lorries installing new machinery at Llanelwedd quarry in the 1920s

In 1910 Thomas Lant reopened it, for there was a growing demand for road stone. In 1928 he sold the concern to The British Quarry Company Ltd, and it is now part of the Amalgamated Roadstone Company. Lant died at his home, 5 Rock Terrace, Llanelwedd, in February 1945 and was buried in Llanelwedd churchyard.

BUILTH IN WARTIME

The Napoleonic Wars were taken seriously in Wales; hard oak from its hills was in greater demand than usual for naval vessels. But in 1813 Builth had rather more direct involvement in the wars than hitherto when the Renfrew Militia halted in the town on its way to the Peninsular. The officers were quartered in the Flag and Castle in the High Street where one of them, it is said, engraved the words 'Renfrew Militia' on a pane of glass in one of the windows. The building, however, was destroyed by fire in 1928.

In 1859 the volunteer movement was established to strengthen home defence, 'to which Palmerston supplied rifles and Tennyson a patriotic poem'. The Builth Volunteers took their responsibilities seriously and in 1866 sought, and received instruction from the Brecknock Militia in drill and musketry. Five years later, in July 1871, Kilvert, who had an affection for Builth, finding 'a glamour and enchantment about the first view of the shining slate roofs . . . and the bridge and the widing reaches of the broad and shining river', had cause, despite 'the beautiful enchantment' he deemed to hang over the town, to record the rather less than 'magical' behaviour of some of its inhabitants:

> This morning Mr Bevan [the vicar of Hay on Wye] went up to the Volunteer Camp above Talgarth on the high common under the Black Mountain. He is chaplain to the forces and intended to hold an open air service and preach a sermon to the Volunteers. . . . When the chaplain arrived on the common, the Builth Volunteers were already well drunk. They were dismissed from the ranks but fought about the common during the whole service. The officers and the other corps were bitterly ashamed and scandalized.

Happily, the Builth Volunteers recovered from their disgrace and their strength was increased to 99 in 1880 under the leadership of Captain M.G. Howell and Dr Bennett of Builth. In 1884 they discarded the distinctive grey uniform which they had worn since 1860 in favour of scarlet, for these were the days before camouflage. Four men of the Builth Volunteers, whose armoury at that time was in West Street, served in the Boer War and their safe return was appropriately celebrated by the town, as were the relief of

The dedication of the incomplete war memorial, 1924

The finished memorial, complete with shaft

Ladysmith in March and of Mafeking in May 1900. The relative importance of these events in local eyes is reflected in the fact that schoolchildren were given a half-day's holiday to celebrate the relief of Ladysmith, but a whole day for the relief of Mafeking, with processions and sports.

The effect of the First World War on the town was far deeper, and the war memorial erected in 1924 commemorates 61 Builth men who, out of a population of some 1,700, were killed in it. During its duration Builth played a part in receiving refugees. Adults collected eggs for the consumption of the wounded at Victoria House Hospital, and children raised money to buy comforts for the sailors. There were daily reminders of the war in the form of heavy coal trains, Jellicoe specials, which enjoyed precedence over all other rail traffic as they rumbled northwards to service the Grand Fleet at Scapa Flow with steam coal from South Wales. Victory was celebrated by a triumphal procession through the town and in 1919 the Endowed School was sent rifles and a helmet as a memento of it all by the Urban District Council. The same year, servicemen returning were treated to a barbecue at the cricket ground, at which the town's butchers provided and cooked the food.

The outbreak of the Second World War in September 1939 saw trenches dug on the Groe and an air-raid shelter constructed on the cricket field. The town, however, was never bombed. A company of the Home Guard formed and met in the Drill Hall to practise first aid and engaged in manoeuvres on

Dr Barnardo's children were evacuated to Builth Wells during the Munich Crisis of 1938

Evacuees from Liverpool arriving at the National School, 1939

the Sugar Loaf, in readiness for invasion by the enemy. The ARP met at the police station to work on air raid precautions, and the church hall was taken over by troops. The scope of war was now total, and even the town's schoolchildren played their part. In 1941 the secondary school formed its own Flight of the Air Training Corps. It also served as a centre for evacuees from bomb-torn Liverpool. Two acres of the playing fields were dug up and cultivated by fourth-form boys inspired by the 'Grow More Food' and 'Dig for Victory' campaigns, while the girls knitted comforts for the troops. Moreover, a staggering £15,000 was invested in war savings by pupils.

The war brought American soldiers to the town. At one time white Americans were stationed at the Pendre Camp in Builth, and black Americans under canvas on a site two miles away at Pencerrig. Relations between the two were not always harmonious and they were kept apart. The black soldiers were not allowed to cross the bridge into the town, and the white Americans were forbidden to cross over from the town side. Skirmishes often resulted when the two groups met. In all, nineteen Builth men died in the Second World War and they are commemorated in a mural tablet set up in the parish church by the Royal British Legion in 1952.

CHAPTER FIVE

Sons and Daughters

Lady Hesther Lucy Stanhope (1776–1839) was the neice of William Pitt. She kept house for him for three years before he died in 1806, gaining a reputation as a brilliant political hostess. During the summer of 1808 she made her way to Builth, where she occupied the Royal Oak (now known as The Lion). Earlier brilliance now gave way to eccentricity. She formed 'some violent attachments to one or two young persons in the place, taking them on long tours on horseback with her through the wild parts of South Wales, their baggage strapped on pack-horses'.

While at Builth Lady Stanhope also displayed enthusiasm as an amateur doctor, vigorously prescribing for the town's sick. In 1808 Lord Kensington and his family were staying in the town at another hotel, where one of his lordship's children had the misfortune to swallow an ear-ring. 'Mercifully or otherwise, Lady Hester was at hand, and took charge of the case, while Builth, with the exception perhaps of the local chirugeon, looked on with admiration and bated breath.' Unfortunately, the outcome of it all is unknown because at this supreme moment the chronicle relating the incident comes suddenly to a stop.

In the spring of 1809 Lady Stanhope established herself at Glan Irfon, a farmhouse on the banks of the Irfon, three miles from the town. Here she kept two saddle horses and a carriage, besides also having a coach at Builth. Before moving to Glan Irfon, besides installing the novelty of a bath (which was apparently soon removed after her departure and used as a granary corn bin), she gave minute written directions as to the colour of her wallpaper, the killing of her mutton, and the mixing of door paint. She hired as her servant a daughter of the Revd John Jones, the vicar of Glascwm from 1787 to 1836, who was no doubt very grateful, for he had thirteen children. Others who were grateful were those who benefited from her distributions of Welsh flannel and cloth.

But Builth's appeal did not last and in 1810 she left Europe for the Orient, where she established herself in a ruined convent at Djoun in the Lebanon. Here, sought out by the distinguished and famous, her eccentricity and her debts increased until she died in 1839.

One of those who enjoyed her favour during her short period at Builth was Thomas Price (1787–1848), who adopted the Welsh bardic name

Thomas Price, 'Carnhuanawc'

Carnhuanawc. He was the son of the vicar of Llanwrthwl, who moved to Builth in 1800. He was for five years at the 'classical school', conducted by the curate, while also coming to the attention of the eccentric Lady Hesther, who was at that time living in the neighbourhood. After his ordination in 1811 Thomas became curate of the Radnorshire parishes of Llanllyr and Llanfihangel Helygen, though he continued to live in Builth. His cottage was on the site of what is now the courtyard of the Greyhound Hotel, and he used to make the journey to the churches that he served on foot. In 1813 he moved to Crickhowel, in the vicinity of which he spent the rest of his life.

Thomas Price, one of the most versatile of men, encouraged the revival of Welsh music, being able both to play and make harps. Price was also a great supporter of the Welsh language and the *eisteddfod*. His monumental *Hanes Cymru*, which appeared in fourteen parts between 1836 and 1842, was for many years the standard history of Wales down to the death of Llywelyn ap Gruffydd in 1282. Price researched the Celtic world, travelled in Brittany, and did much to foster an interest in Celtic history, antiquities and languages. But for all his wealth of scholarship he remained a faithful pastor all his life, and when he died *The Hereford Times* remembered him as 'a living example of what the human mind can accomplish *unaided*, with no great advantages of education, without patronage, without rank, or connexions, without more than income sufficient to procure what would generally be called the bare necessaries of life.'

Thomas Jeffery Llewelyn Prichard (1790–1862), probably knew both Lady Stanhope and Thomas Price. He was born at Builth but left Wales in boyhood. He earned his living first as an actor in London, but having returned to Wales he seems to have settled for a while at Aberystwyth. Then, in January 1826 he married Naomi James of Builth and for some years lived in the town as a bookseller, his daughter Serena carrying on the business after him. Though an indifferent poet he is still remembered as the author of *The Adventures and Vagaries of Twm Shôn Catti*, first published in 1828. He was still in Builth in 1839, but he returned to the life of a strolling actor and suffered disfigurement when he lost his nose in a fencing accident.

He wrote several guidebooks, including *The Cambria Balnea: or Guide to the Watering Places of Wales, Marine and Inland*, 1825. Here he describes with appropriate lyricism the turnpike road between Rhaeadr and Builth which ran, as does its modern successor, for almost the whole of the way along the banks of the Wye. 'The scenery is often strikingly beautiful, with considerable

The Castle, childhood home of Hilda Vaughan

variation from craggy promontories and barren wilds, to grassy dells, occasionally graced with sturdy forest trees and young plantations of ever-green pines and larches, forming a chaplet . . . to beautify even the sullen brows of winter.' All this would yield the traveller 'fine scope for his muse, pencil, or contemplation'. Prichard died at Swansea, after another disastrous accident in which he fell into his livingroom fire and was fatally burned. He is commemorated in a sculpture in the quadrangle of Builth High School.

The most distinguished literary figure, however, connected with Builth was Hilda Vaughan (1892–1985). She deserves, we are told, 'to be remembered as the writer who derived her inspiration from the upper middle-Wye valley and from the country and people around it. Sadly her name is over-looked by the compilers of literary atlases.' She was the daughter of Hugh Vaughan Vaughan (1852–1937), a Builth solicitor.

Hilda Vaughan was born in Builth and spent her childhood at The Castle, one of the lost houses of Wales, having been demolished in 1974. Built in the seventeenth century, it was enlarged by Lord James Vaughan on his marriage to one of the Harley family. It was further rebuilt in the nineteenth century when in the 1860s her uncle (who eventually left it to her father), 'added plate-glass bow windows to our house and stuck castellated battlements upon the roof and made other grandiose improvements in the taste of his own age'. She remembered with particular pleasure, though, its 'gracefully curved staircase of dark polished oak'.

Hilda Vaughan's first published novel, *The Battle to the Weak* (1925) was set largely near Builth and followed by several other novels and plays. Her autobiographical essay *Far away: Not Long Ago* contains a description of a journey into Builth in the family dog-cart, hauled by Taffy their pony:

We executed a right-angle turn on one wheel into the main street, just missing the butchers' dogs and preceded by our own, who tore ahead of us, frantically barking. Everyone in the place stood conversing in the middle of the roadway. They sprang on to the pavement only when Taffy's foam-splashed blinkers were close upon them. Grinning, they touched their hats to my father, who turned round to wave friendly salutations. Every time he did this, Taffy shied from gutter to gutter, and we were nearly flung off our narrow perch. On market days the street was full of cattle. It had not been thought necessary to build a smithfield, since folk were in no hurry to pass through the town. Cows, guarding their calves, rushed with horns lowered at our dogs. Flocks of sheep brought us to a series of abrupt halts, while Taffy danced with impatience.

Index